Amazing Animals
Cats

Please visit our web site at www.garethstevens.com
For a free catalog describing our list of high-quality books, call 1-800-542-2595 (USA) or 1-800-387-3178 (Canada).
Our fax: 1-877-542-2596

Library of Congress Cataloging-in-Publication Data

Wilsdon, Christina.
    Cats / by Christina Wilsdon.—U.S. ed.
        p. cm. — (Amazing Animals)
        Originally published: Pleasantville, NY: Reader's Digest Young Families, c2007.
        Includes bibliographical references and index.
        ISBN-10: 0-8368-9105-8   ISBN-13: 978-0-8368-9105-8 (lib. bdg.)
        ISBN-10: 1-4339-2022-0   ISBN-13: 978-1-4339-2022-6 (soft cover)
    1. Cats—Juvenile literature. I. Title.
    SF445.7.W54 2009
    636.8—dc22   2008027900

This edition first published in 2009 by
Gareth Stevens Publishing
A Weekly Reader® Company
1 Reader's Digest Road
Pleasantville, NY 10570-7000 USA

This edition copyright © 2009 by Gareth Stevens, Inc. Original edition copyright © 2007 by Reader's Digest Young Families, Pleasantville, NY 10570

Gareth Stevens Executive Managing Editor: Lisa M. Herrington
Gareth Stevens Creative Director: Lisa Donovan
Gareth Stevens Art Director: Ken Crossland
Gareth Stevens Associate Editor: Amanda Hudson
Gareth Stevens Publisher: Keith Garton

Consultant: Robert E. Budliger (Retired), NY State Department of Environmental Conservation

Photo Credits
Front cover: Dreamstime.com/Marilyn Barbone, Title page: iStockphoto.com, Contents page: iStockphoto.com/Tina Rencelj, pages 6-7: iStockphoto.com/Lauri Wiberg, page 8: iStockphoto.com/Arkadiusz Stachowski, page 11: Dreamstime.com/Stephanie Dankof, page 12: Dreamstime.com/Matthew Skretting, pages 14-15: iStockphoto.com/Joeilen Armstrong, page 16: Dreamstime.com/Simone Van Den Berg, page 19: Jill Bauman, page 20: Dreamstime.com/Joshua Laymon, page 21: iStockphoto.com/Sergey Kashkin, pages 22-23: Dreamstime.com/Norman Chan, page 24: Image Source, page 26: Dreamstime.com/Igor Zhorov, page 27: Dreamstime.com/Claudia Van der Sluis, page 28: Dreamstime.com/Andrew Obrezkov, pages 30-31: Dreamstime.com, page 32: iStockphoto.com/Jeremy Viosey, page 35: Dreamstime.com/Kathy Dyer, page 36: Dreamstime.com/Petr Nad, pages 38-39: iStockphoto.com/Misha Shiyanov, page 40: Shawn Hine/Shutterstock.com Inc. page 43: Brad Whitsitt/Shutterstock.com Inc., pages 44-45: Dreamstime.com/Francisco javier Alcerreca Gomez.

Every effort has been made to trace the copyright holders for the photos used in this book, and the publisher apologizes in advance for any unintentional omissions. We would be pleased to insert the appropriate acknowledgements in any subsequent edition of this publication.

Printed in the United States of America

1 2 3 4 5 6 7 8 9 13 12 11 10 09

Amazing Animals
Cats

By Christina Wilsdon

 **Gareth Stevens**
Publishing

Contents

Chapter 1
A Cat Story

Cat Words

A female cat is called a **queen**. A male cat is called a **tom**. Baby cats are called **kittens**. A female cat can have one to nine kittens in a **litter**.

A mother cat slipped into a closet. She climbed into a box with a blanket. She pushed at the blanket with her paws until she had made a cozy nest. The box had been set up for her by her owners. It was the perfect spot for giving birth to her babies.

A few hours later, five tiny kittens shared the box with the mother cat. She licked the kittens from head to toe.

One of the baby cats felt his mother's rough tongue on his fur. But he could not see her. His eyes were shut. His ears were folded against his head, so he could not hear her, either. All he could do was smell her.

The baby cat wriggled closer to his mother. Soon he was drinking her milk. His brothers and sisters tumbled over him to reach her, too.

As the kittens nursed, the mother cat **purred**. She was tired but happy. The kittens were tired, too. They huddled together to keep warm.

Each day the baby cat's eyes opened a little bit more. By the time he was eight days old, he was able to look at the world.

Another week passed. Now the baby cat was ready to creep away from his mother. He got to the side of the box and started to climb out. His mother grabbed him by the scruff of his neck and gently pulled him back in.

The baby cat was still small, but he now weighed three times as much as when he was born. His only food was his mother's milk. He drank the milk from the same spot on her belly every day. If one of his brothers or sisters took his spot, he shoved and squirmed until he got it back.

By the time he was three weeks old, the baby cat was out of the box for most of the day. He explored with the other kittens. The mother cat always kept an eye on them.

Baby Blues

A kitten's eyes are always blue at birth. By the time it is about 12 weeks old, its eyes start changing to the color they will be for the rest of its life.

Lots of Company

A female cat can have one to nine kittens in a **litter**. The usual number is between three and five.

Time to Go

A kitten is ready to leave its mother and go to a new home when it is about 10 weeks old.

When the baby cat was about six weeks old, he was zipping around the house with his brothers and sisters. When he grabbed hold of another kitten, the two of them would roll around like a fuzzy ball.

One day the kittens knocked over a plant. It landed with a crash! But their owner cleaned it up. Then she cuddled the kittens. The baby cat and the other kittens trusted the people in the house. Being handled gently by people would help them be good pets when they grew up.

The mother cat watched over her kittens. She knew they would not hurt each other. The chasing and tumbling was just play. It was good exercise for the kittens' growing muscles.

The baby cat learned a lot during his first few weeks of life. He learned to groom his own fur and how to use a **litter box**. He also decided that cat food tasted great!

The baby cat will stop drinking the mother cat's milk when he is about two months old. He will eat cat food after that. He will be fully grown when he is about a year old.

Chapter 2
The Body of a Cat

Wild Words

The word **feline** is from the Latin word *feles*, which means "cat."

The feline family includes all cats, big and small—from huge Siberian tigers to the tiniest house cats.

Cat Cousins

House cats and lions belong to the same group of animals called the feline family. Like all felines, the house cat is a **carnivore** (CAR nih vor). That means it is a meat-eater. A house cat is built for hunting.

The bones in a house cat's back are connected less tightly to one another than those of other animals. This makes a cat's backbone very flexible. A house cat can easily move its body to climb, jump, and run. If you have ever watched a cat twist while washing itself, you've seen how flexible it is!

Go, Cat, Go

A cat walks by moving both legs on one side of its body. Then it moves the legs on the other side. Camels and giraffes are the only other animals to move this way. A cat's paw prints form almost a straight line.

A running cat bounds on its two hind legs. It lands first on one front paw, then the other. A cat easily jumps up to high perches and walks on narrow ledges. It climbs up a tree headfirst and comes down the trunk backward. If it falls, a cat twists its head and then its body so that it lands safely on its feet.

Eyes

A cat's eyes sit at the front of its head, like yours do. This gives it the kind of vision it needs to judge how far away things are—a skill it needs to pounce on a mouse.

A cat can see six times better than you can in dim light. The dark pupil in the middle of a cat's eye opens into a wide circle to let in light. Light also bounces off the inside back of each eye. This gives the cat a second chance to use some of the light to help it see. It also makes a cat's eyes glow in the dark when you shine a flashlight at it!

Whiskers

Sprouting from either side of a cat's face are long, stiff hairs called whiskers. A typical cat has about 24 whiskers. It also has whiskery hairs above its eyes, around its face, and on its legs.

A cat's whiskers are sensitive. They are connected to the brain by many nerves and can detect even the slightest motion of air. This helps a cat find its way in the dark.

A cat can move the whiskers on its snout forward and back. A cat's close-up vision is poor. Feeling with its whiskers helps the cat find things that it can't see.

Super Hearing

A cat can hear very high-pitched sounds, like the squeaking of mice. It moves its ears in all directions to listen for sounds. Many pet cats will run to the door long before a visitor even gets there!

A cat's eyes are so beautiful that some gems are known as "cat's eyes."

Sharp Tongue

Have you ever been licked by a friendly cat? Then you know that a cat's tongue feels rough. It is covered with bumps. The bumps let a cat lick small bits of meat off a bone. The roughness also helps a cat groom its fur.

A cat usually has five toes on each front paw and four toes on each hind paw. Sometimes cats are born with extra toes.

Teeth ...

An adult cat has 30 teeth. The biggest teeth are the four long fangs called canines. These teeth are used to grab and kill **prey**. They also help tear apart meat.

In between the top and bottom canines are twelve little teeth called incisors. A cat uses these to nibble food.

Behind the fangs are sharp teeth called **carnassials** (car NAS ee uls). These pointy teeth work like scissors. A cat turns its head sideways to slice food with its carnassials.

... And Claws!

Each cat toe has a sharp **claw**. A cat uses its claws to hold prey, to climb, and to protect itself. They are kept hidden inside the cat's paws. This helps keep the claws sharp. Claws that stick out would get worn down.

A cat's claws pop out when a cat attacks or defends itself. This happens when the cat tightens muscles in its legs. The cat's toes spread apart at the same time. You can see this when a cat stretches after a nap.

Chapter 3
What Cats Do

You can see hunting behavior by watching a cat at play. It will stalk and pounce upon a blade of grass or a wiggling string. Some cats will even chase the beam of a flashlight!

Surprise Attacks

A domestic cat hunts the same way that a wild cat does. It sneaks up on its prey. This is called stalking. A stalking cat crouches down and slinks low to the ground. If it thinks it has been spotted by its prey, it stands still until its prey relaxes. When the cat is close to its prey, it charges.

Cats play with other cats if they know them well. Kittens stalk and pounce on each other. Grown-up cats play less. But they will also stalk friends and wrestle or play with their owners. Some cats like to launch surprise attacks on people's ankles as they walk by!

Claw Care

Claws become dull with use. Cats use their teeth to pull off the outer layer of each claw to uncover a new, sharp layer underneath.

Many people think a cat is sharpening its claws when it hooks them into a tree and scratches. Actually, the cat does this to stretch its muscles. But the action does help to remove the claws' old outer layers. Clawing is also a way for the cat to leave its scent on the tree for other cats to smell.

Keeping Clean

A cat may spend half of its waking hours grooming itself. It licks its fur with its raspy tongue, which works like a comb. Licking also spreads oils made in the cat's skin across its fur. These oils give a cat's fur its shine. The oils also contain scents that the cat uses to mark its **territory** by rubbing against objects.

A cat's body is so flexible that it can reach almost every part of its body as it grooms. It can even twist its neck to lick its own shoulders! A cat uses its teeth to pull snarls out of its fur and dirt out of its paws.

Cats also groom each other. A female cat licks her kittens. Cats that live together often lick each other. Some cats try to "groom" their owners!

Cat Naps

A cat may rest up to 14 hours a day. An old cat or a cat living in a hot climate may rest more!

To wash its face, a cat first licks its front paws. Then it rubs the wet paw over its ears and on its face.

Sniff!

Cats mark their territory by rubbing their scent onto objects. A cat does this by rubbing its chin, the sides of its face, or even its whole body against different things—such as a tree, a chair, or your leg!

This cat's meow may mean "let me in," "look at me," or "where's the cat food?"

Cat Talk

A cat meows to get attention. It purrs when it is content. Female cats purr to their kittens, and kittens purr as they nurse. Many cats purr when they are stroked. Oddly, a nervous cat may also purr.

Cats use other sounds when they are upset. An angry or fearful cat growls and hisses. A very angry cat can make a noise that sounds like a scream.

Body Language

A cat's ears, whiskers, and tail can show how a cat is feeling. A friendly cat pricks up its ears, holds its tail up straight, and points its whiskers forward. A fearful cat folds back its ears and whiskers. An annoyed cat lashes its tail.

A cat uses its body to express itself. It may greet its owner by rolling over and showing its belly. But an aggressive cat approaches with ears folded back, back arched, and fur puffed up. A fearful cat holds its ears out sideways. It may arch its back and puff up its fur.

Cats often begin a fight by staring at each other. A scared cat's pupils grow round and large. A relaxed cat may close its eyes halfway.

Chapter 4
Kinds of Cats

Cat Breeds

A cat that belongs to a special **breed** has a certain kind of fur, shape, or color that it shares with other cats of the same breed. Cat breeds are divided into two main groups: **short-haired** breeds and **long-haired** breeds.

Short-Haired Cats

Short-haired breeds are usually divided into two groups. One group is simply called shorthairs. The other group is called foreign, or Oriental, shorthairs. Foreign shorthairs have leaner bodies and thinner, wedge-shaped heads than other shorthairs.

The **British shorthair** is a round-faced, sturdy cat. Its cousin, the **American shorthair**, is a relative of the cats that helped the early settlers control mice and rats on their farms.

The **Siamese cat** is one of the most popular foreign shorthairs. A Siamese has long, thin legs and a long tail, which are darker than its body. The Siamese's face and ears are darker, too. Siamese cats are famous for yowling!

Other foreign shorthairs include the **Korat**, with its thick fur of bluish silver, and the all-black **Bombay**.

Long-Haired Cats

The first long-haired cats, which came from Asia, were brought to Europe about 500 years ago. Over time, these cats were bred to produce new long-haired breeds.

One of these breeds is the **Angora**. Its fur is long and fluffy. In summer, it sheds a lot. The first Angoras were white, but today Angoras come in many colors.

Another long-haired breed is the **Persian**. The first Persian cats came from Iran, which was once called Persia. A Persian cat has long outer fur. Under this long hair is a fuzzy undercoat. All this fur makes a Persian look plump.

Other long-haired breeds include **Birmans**, **Turkish Vans**, and **Maine Coon** cats.

Good Looks Take Work

Long-haired cats need to be brushed to keep their fur clean. Brushing also keeps the fur free of tangled clumps, called mats.

Just Cats!

Most pet cats are a mixture of breeds. A veterinarian may call a cat like this a domestic shorthair, a domestic longhair, or a mixed breed. Most people simply call them house cats.

Persian cats, like this one, have flatter faces and shorter noses than Angoras.

Chocolate Cats?

Cat breeders use different words to describe cats' colors. A dark-gray cat is said to be **blue**. A pale-gray cat is lilac or lavender. A tan cat is called cream. An orange cat is called a red cat. A brown cat may be called chocolate, while a reddish brown one is called cinnamon.

A calico is not a breed of cat — it is the color pattern of the cat's coat.

Colorful Kitties

Cats' coats come in a variety of colors and patterns. A cat can be all one color—black, white, red, or gray. A cat whose coat has two solid colors is called a **bicolor**.

Many bicolors are splashed with large patches of color and white. One bicolor is the tuxedo cat. A tuxedo cat has a black body and tail, white paws, and a white belly.

Tricolor cats have three colors. Tortoiseshell cats have red, cream, and black hairs. A tortoiseshell cat is often called a **tortie**. If it has striped markings mixed in, it is called a torbie. One of the patterns is called tortie-and-white, or calico. A calico cat has patches of black, red, and cream or white.

Stripes, Spots, and Points

Striped cats are called tabby cats. Tabby markings can also include rows of spots. Many wild **species** of cats are also striped or spotted.

Cats with pale bodies and dark legs, faces, ears, and tails are called **colorpoint** cats. Siamese cats are colorpoint cats.

Chapter 5
Cats in the World

Cats and People

The ancestor of the domestic cat is thought to be the African wildcat. This cat lives in parts of Africa and the Middle East. It preys on small animals, insects, and birds.

Nobody knows where or when the first wildcat was tamed. But people have kept cats as pets for nearly 5,000 years.

In ancient Egypt, cats earned respect by getting rid of mice and rats that lived in grain bins. The ancient Egyptians worshipped cats. After cats died, they were wrapped in linen and made into mummies.

Good Luck, Bad Luck

For the past 2,000 years, cats and humans have shared an up-and-down history. Sometimes people treated cats well. People in parts of France believed some cats were magic. If the cats were treated nicely, they brought good luck. In China, people thought cats could chase away evil spirits.

At other times, people feared cats. Many cats were killed in Europe starting in the 1400s. People thought they were evil spirits.

The Future of Cats

Cats are very popular as pets. Today, there are more than 90 million pet cats in the United States alone!

One problem with pet cats is that when they roam outdoors, they sometimes kill large numbers of birds and other small animals. On some islands, cats have caused certain kinds of birds to become rare or even extinct. Pet owners are often encouraged to keep their cats indoors.

Another problem is cat overpopulation. There are too many cats and not enough homes for them all. Millions of cats are brought into animal shelters each year. Many people help prevent cat overpopulation by spaying or neutering their cats. These operations stop cats from having kittens. This gives cats who are already living in shelters a better chance at finding a new home—where they can become somebody's "purr-fect" pet.

Fast Facts About House Cats

Scientific name	*Felis catus*
Class	Mammalia
Order	Carnivora
Size	Up to 10 inches (25 cm) tall at the shoulder
Weight	Up to 20 pounds (9 kilograms)
Life span	Up to 20 years

Glossary

bicolor — a cat that has a coat of two solid colors

blue — a word for any dark-gray cat

breed — a specific kind of cat

carnassials — teeth used for slicing meat

carnivore — a meat-eating animal

claws — a cat's sharp nails

colorpoint — a cat with legs, ears, tail, and face darker than the body

kitten — a baby cat

litter — a group of kittens born at the same time

litter box — a box containing gravel or other materials that a cat uses as a toilet

long-haired — a category of cat breeds that have long hair

prey — animals that are hunted by other animals for food

purr — a rumbling sound often made by a contented cat

queen — a female cat

short-haired — a category of cat breeds that have short hair

species — a group of living things that are the same in many ways

territory — an area of land that an animal marks as its own

tom — a male cat

tortie — another word for a tortoiseshell cat

Cats: Show What You Know

How much have you learned about cats? Grab a piece of paper and a pencil and write your answers down.

1. What is another name for a male cat?

2. What color are a kitten's eyes at birth?

3. At what age is a kitten ready to leave its mother and go to a new home?

4. Why is a cat's backbone so flexible?

5. How many whiskers does a typical cat have?

6. How do cats mark their territory?

7. What does it usually mean when a cat lashes its tail?

8. What are the two main groups of cat breeds?

9. Where did the first long-haired cats come from?

10. What is another name for a striped cat?

1. A tom 2. Blue 3. About 10 weeks 4. Because the bones are connected less tightly than those of other animals 5. About 24 6. By rubbing their scent onto objects 7. It is annoyed! 8. Short-haired and long-haired 9. Asia 10. Tabby cat

For More Information

Books

Everything Cat: What Kids Really Want to Know About Cats. Kids' FAQs (series). Crisp, Marty (NorthWord Press, 2003)

How to Talk to Your Cat. George, Jean Craighead (HarperTrophy, 2003)

Why Do Cats Meow? Easy-to-Read (series). Holub, Joan (Puffin, 2001)

Web Sites

ASPCA Animaland Cat Care

www.aspca.org/site/PageServer?pagename=kids_pc_cat_411

Find out basic facts about cats and how to care for them. You can also click on a link to watch pet care cartoons.

Cats International

www.catsinternational.org

Check out the library of articles on this educational organization's web site dedicated to helping people better understand their cats.

Publisher's note to educators and parents: Our editors have carefully reviewed these web sites to ensure that they are suitable for children. Many web sites change frequently, however, and we cannot guarantee that a site's future contents will continue to meet our high standards of quality and educational value. Be advised that children should be closely supervised whenever they access the Internet.

Index